D0621606

ROBERT CAPA

Robert Capa

Introduction by
Jean Lacouture
Translation by
Abigail Pollak

PANTHEON BOOKS, NEW YORK

CENTRE NATIONAL DE LA PHOTOGRAPHIE, PARIS

On the cover: Death of a Republican Soldier, Spain, 1936.

Library of Congress Cataloging-in-Publication Data

Capa, Robert, 1913-1954.
(Robert Capa, English)
Robert Capa / Introduction by Jean Lacouture; translated by Abigail Pollak
p.cm.
Translated from the French.
Bibliography: p.
ISBN 0-679-72336-6
1. Photography, Artistic. 2. Capa, Robert, 1913-1954.
I. Lacouture, Jean. II. Centre national de la photographie (France). III.
Title.TR654.C34413   1989
799'.092'4   88–43242

First American Edition / Manufactured in Italy

TOWARD PHOTO-HISTORY

Legendary – how to avoid this word so often used to describe Robert Capa? Like that of the actor, the profession of pursuer of pictures, and facts, is fraught with an onerous and sometimes demeaning mythology. With the exception of Molière, however, few actors have died onstage, whereas countless photographers – Capa foremost – have given their lives in an effort to get a firmer grip on the truth.

The legend of the founder of Magnum Photos is more than a tale of office girls and shutterbugs. We who have gone the same route, who have "followed the leader" (like Brassens's little pony), have made of this story an inspiring myth. After all, why shouldn't we dare what he dared? Why shouldn't we ourselves try to capture what he captured – in Spain, China, and Sicily, during the Normandy invasion, and in Indochina?.

Of course, the man with the camera in his hand faces far more rigorous imperatives than the pen-pusher. His highest credo – "being there" – is both more tyrannical and more all-consuming than ours. He must get closer, ever closer... and indeed, Capa's greatest scoops imply a dizzying proximity. (It's no accident that the two people dearest to him, Gerda Taro and David "Chim" Seymour, died exactly as he did.) For those of us hidng behind our little pads and pencils, Bob Capa's example has proved both thrilling and seductive. He spurred us forward, prodded us ever onward toward the truth. This man, whom I never had the pleasure of knowing personally – my assignments in Indochina came before and after his tragic death in 1954 – has been a compelling motivator, not only in my life but in the lives of so many others, perhaps even more after his death than during his lifetime.

André Friedmann was born in 1911, to a middle-class family in Budapest (I wonder if we've sufficiently acknowledged photography's debt to Hungary, from Kertész to Brassaï, Munkacsi to Capa, and so many others?). He was a good student, a high-strung adolescent involved in revolutionary political groups inspired by Lajos Kassák. For a young and exuberant Jew, these were difficult times, anti-Semitism being the rule rather than the exception. In 1931, André was forced to flee to Berlin, where he was taken in by another Hungarian, Simon Guttmann, the founder of the Dephot Agency (Deutsche Photodienst) and the father of modern photojournalism. At that time, there was no waiting for André to prove himself; he was immediately sent to Copenhagen, where Trotsky, with Stalin in hot pursuit, was to give a speech. From that moment, Capa lived with a camera in his hand, even when the advent of Nazism forced him to leave Berlin.

He fled, of course, to Paris, to the Montparnasse of the 1930s, and was instantly seduced. The fierce nomad, the traveler always camping out in temporary quarters, the wanderer who would never have a favorite hotel in New York or London or Hong Kong, fell in love with Paris, which was at the time – if we're to believe Hemingway – a movable feast. One must remember, however, that to see Paris as a perpetual party was harder for a Hungarian refugee than for an American writer; the fate of Jews from Eastern Europe, who lived under the watchful eye of Monsieur Chiappe's police, was not an enviable one.

The newcomers supported one another and created organizations for mutual aid. During one of their meetings, André met a small and rather delicate man, shy but jovial, his eyes hidden behind thick spectacles, a Pole by the name of David Szymin. They immediately struck up a friendship, and a pact was sealed between the daring Hungarian loner with the velvet-black eyes and the skinny student from the Orthodox Jewish community in Warsaw, the latter haunted by the tragic fate of the Jewish people, the former proclaiming cheerfully that no curse exists that cannot be swept away by courage and an enterprising spirit.

This wonderful alliance with "Chim," a partnership that gave André's short and violent life a halo of human gentleness, would be followed by five crucial discoveries: Gerda, Henri, the Leica, the war, and – "Robert Capa."

Gerda Taro was a twenty-year-old German student, slender, blond, and a fearless anti-Fascist. She was the great love of André's life and the best of his colleagues, but would die young in Spain, crushed by a Republican tank on the Brunete Front. André never really recovered from the wrenching anguish of her death; his first book, *Death in the Making*, about the war against Franco, was signed by both of them.

A few years after their friendship began, Chim introduced André to the Dôme, the café-restaurant in Montparnasse where Anaïs Nin gazed soulfully into Henry Miller's eyes and Aragon read aloud to Philippe Soupault from *Le paysan de Paris*. On certain nights, Chim and André were joined by a tall young man with a high forehead, a bold look, and a voice filled with passion; this was Henri Cartier-Bresson, still straddling the fence between Surrealism and intergalactic adventure, Cubist painting and his camera. With one stroke, the little Polish refugee forged an alliance between the decade's two most antithetical pursuers of the image – movement and structure, nature and culture – a partnership as improbable as that of the torrent and the rock.

The formation of this trio, brought together so magically in Montparnasse, might not have proved so fruitful, however, had it not been for the timely appearance of the Leica, the perfect instrument for the venture they were just beginning to formulate. The Leica had been adopted only recently by André Kertész, but would prove to do for photojournalism what Guibert's invention of the division did for Napoleon. An extension of the arm, friend of the eye, perfect for the direct, fast, and surreptitious glance, creator of lines and inventor of visual understatement, the Leica transformed the trio conceived at the Dôme in 1934 into a quartet.

All that remained was the right occasion, the chance to prove, with a brilliant display, the power of this new instrument to capture life. The opportunity presented itself in 1935, first in Ethiopia and Manchuria, then in Spain, and then in the great French popular demonstrations of 1936, when the frenzied world offered photojournalism an incomparable booty in the form of chaos, madness, martyrdom, and opéra-bouffe.

André's fifth conquest was "Robert Capa." The origins of this pseudonym are unclear; perhaps the Hungarian word for "sword," or the Spanish word for cape, or disguise, or even the slightly altered name of the great director Frank Capra, whom André admired above all others, according to his biographer, Richard Whelan. In any case, it seems a perfect pseudonym – international, pronounceable in all languages, a name André cleverly used in his role of the "great American photographer," referring to "Friedmann," in Paris, as his representative while speaking glowingly, as Capa in New York, of his "friend André."

It was Capa then, Bob Capa, whose photographs of the Spanish Civil War spread like wildfire around the world. The most famous shot any photographer had yet taken with his little black box appeared in 1936, the photo of a Republican soldier in white work clothes, pale as Cocteau's angel, falling backward, struck down on a hillside, his rifle blown from his grasp by the fiery breath of death. Even when people no longer know anything about this war or what it meant for the future of the world, they will still stare, transfixed, at this incredible image. All our writing may vanish, like the hieroglyphics after Emperor Theodosius's interdiction, but this photograph will remain a sort of ideograph of the war.

During the summer of 1938, just after the death of Gerda, the now-famous Capa found himself in China. Simon Guttmann, Capa's former patron from Berlin who had also fled to Paris, had organized the operation, forming a pool which included *Life* magazine, Agence Pix, and the pro-Communist weekly *Clartés*. Capa wrote from Hangchow to an old Hungarian friend; he could no longer endure his present situation, the way Guttmann treated Capa's talent, his trips, his very life, as his own property. Out of this discontent came the idea of smashing the tyranny of the "bosses" and the newspaper cartels by creating a cooperative agency, to be formed by Capa, Chim, and Cartier-Bresson. Here, Capa was clearly influenced by his experience with the Popular Front, which saw the flowering of so many cooperatives, including the one evoked by Jean Renoir in *The Crime of Monsieur Lange*.

In his memoirs, Capa wrote that he found himself in New York at the end of 1942, out of work and up to his ears in debt. One morning, between the rent and telephone bills that had been slipped under his door, Capa found a letter from *Collier's* magazine offering him the chance to cover the war in Europe. Eighteen months later he emerged from the blood-soaked dust of Tunisia, the chaos in Sicily and Rome, the waves of troops landing on the beaches of Normandy, and found a Paris laughing through its tears, a Paris corrupted but free, defiled but marvelous, a summertime Paris, war-torn but feverish with joy. He entered the city, to great adulation, at the head of a host of friends – John Huston, William Saroyan,

Irwin Shaw, George Stevens, Ernest Hemingway – followed soon afterward by Chim, now known as Seymour, and expecting Cartier-Bresson to leap out at any moment from behind some barricade or other.

Robert Capa was now thirty-three. To have an idea of what he must have been like during those prodigious time at the Dôme or at the bar of the Ritz, requires us to imagine someone with the energy of Joseph Kessel, the swagger and audacity of Erroll Flynn, the sparkling fantasy of the young Yves Montand, and the cheerful compulsiveness of Ernest Hemingway. In Robert Capa, people saw the character who inspired Clark Gable, the reporter-hero in *Too Hot to Handle*, which was shot on the eve of the war. (What a marvelous Capa Robert De Niro would make today!)

Saroyan described Capa as "basically a poker player who took pictures on the side." Throughout Africa, Italy, France, and the Ardennes, however, he captured more moments of life and death with his camera than any man of his time, and this without loving any fewer women or losing any less money at cards than those who competed with him for the number-one slot. He was fearless, isolent, and extravagant. He seemed to live with more intensity than anyone else, capturing the heart of Ingrid Bergman, among others.

Capa's 1938 Hangchow dream of a cooperative agency became reality in April of 1947, in the restaurant of the Museum of Modern Art in New York. The founding members were Robert Capa, Henri Cartier-Bresson, Chim Seymour, George Rodger (not present at the MOMA meeting), and William and Rita Vandivert, who left the group soon afterward. On May 22, 1947, Magnum Photos received a commercial license from the city and was ready for business.

Where did that proud and noble Roman name, Magnum, come from? Among a dozen other associations in Capa's mind, the word Magnum evoked the word champagne. Every one of the agency's innumerable successes had to be celebrated, at least until the founder's death, with the pop of one of those voluptuously shaped bottles.

The question remains as to why these men chose to form a co-op. When the idea first came to Capa in China, these photojournalists were still on salary but already famous. Throughout the war, they continued to prove their masterful superiority, and were clearly in a position to challenge the dictates of the press bosses. Why then did they opt to create an organization that by definition would impose all sorts of other demands – the pooling of their work, the administration of a collective patrimony – on this group of individualists, these lone wolves plying the trade of photojournalist?

In response, Romeo Martinez explains: "Capa's idea – specifically, that the journalist is nothing if he doesn't own his own negatives – will prove to be the sanest idea in the history of photojournalism. The co-op is the best formula for retaining those rights, and for ensuring the freedom of action of each of its members."

The creation of Magnum in 1947 changed nothing in Capa's life style or professional activities. In his role of co-op "president" he supplied most of the grist for the mill, coming up with a dozen ideas an hour, scolding and hustling his associates, tossing out constant challenges, bluffing, provoking, exasperating, endangering the very existence of the agency with his gambling debts and lavish expense accounts, then rescuing it with some new feat of derring-do, or simply with his genius for business. In fact, with every passing day Capa seemed more impatient to surpass his fame as a devourer of images, of risks... and of women. "A gambler? Perhaps. But at least he's not a cheater!" said Marc Riboud, who worked closely with him at the time and knew him well. Indeed, at the height of his fame Capa seemed to be everywhere – in Israel with Irwin Shaw, in Poland, in Morocco, shooting portraits of Picasso, Matisse, the Aga Khan, Eisenhower.

For seven years, men had been dying in Indochina for reasons no one seemed to understand very well. Capa's problem was not so much the why but the how. He despised war; it had taken Gerda from him, as well as many of his friends, not to mention most of his illusions. Yet war was an integral part of his world, and the source of his fame. How could he let the war in Indochina run its course without taking a look at it? His friends at Magnum warned him: Why be in such a hurry to leave? They asked. And did he really want to impose that trial upon himself? The answer was yes, and when Capa boarded a plane for Saigon in the spring of 1954 it was neither an act of bravado nor a moment of thoughtless caprice.

The month of May found him in Hanoi. The fall of Dien Bien Phu came on the seventh, but the fighting continued. Capa decided to join a contingent headed for Thai Binh. On the twenty-fifth, he left the road in order to get a clearer shot of the soldiers and stepped on a mine. He died a few minutes later, one leg blown off. His mother vetoed the honors proposed by the French army to commemorate his death; there would be no military homage for this man who despised war.

If the photograph is life, then Capa was photography. In fact, for him photography was more than that, which was why he needed Chim's conscience and Cartier-Bresson's sense of aesthetic structure. Yet Capa's contributions – motivation, energy, imagination – were no less vital to Magnum's success, or to the growth of modern photojournalism.

Had it not been for fascism and the war, André Friedmann, nicknamed "Bandi," might have been an energetic young businessman from Pest. Or the founder of a shipping company on the Danube, or an orchestra, or a theater in Buda. Whichever, he would surely have astonished the world he lived in and shaken up the world at large.

What he shook up, indeed turned upside down, was the act of photography. In freeing his friends at Magnum from the tyranny of the big magazines and agencies that had always owned not only their photographers' time but their negatives, Capa invented a wholly new method of giving chase to the image.

Early in 1954, Robert Capa told Marc Riboud that the development of television posed a real danger to photojournalism. This danger has now clearly been surmonted, despite the ongoing need for research and reconversion. If the reign of television has in any way altered the profession of photography, however, it is in the conquest of time and duration. Like their colleagues in the press, perhaps photographers will increasingly tend to detach themselves from the moment and concentrate on notions of permanence and sequence. And history – as progression, and as both a reshaping of the world and a struggle against forgetting. Like so many others since then, both Capa and Magnum, in their pursuit of photo-history, have pointed the way.

Jean Lacouture
Translated by Abigail Pollak

1. Trotsky's speech on the history of the Russian Revolution, Copenhagen, November 27, 1932.

2. Paris, 1936.

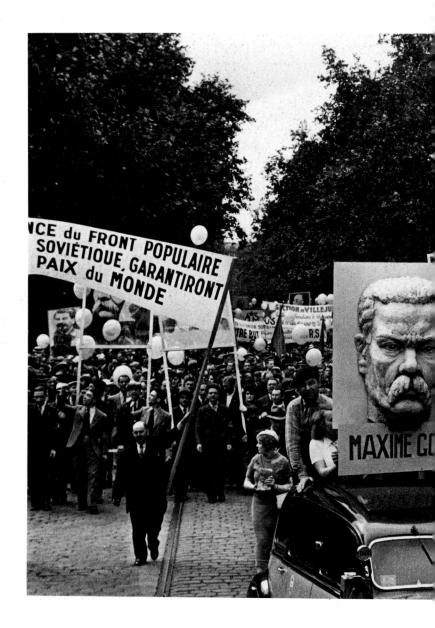

3. Paris, July 14, 1936.

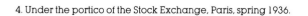
4. Under the portico of the Stock Exchange, Paris, spring 1936.

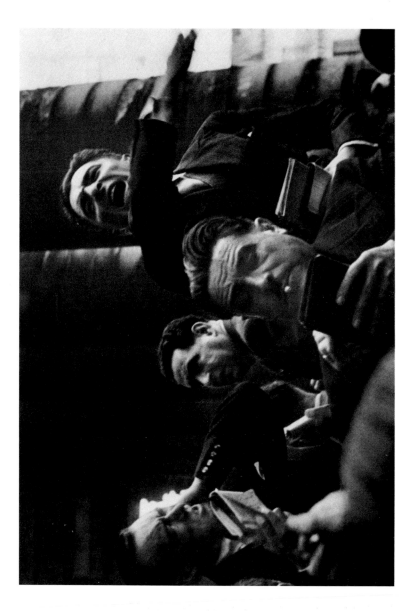

5. Paris, May 1, 1937.

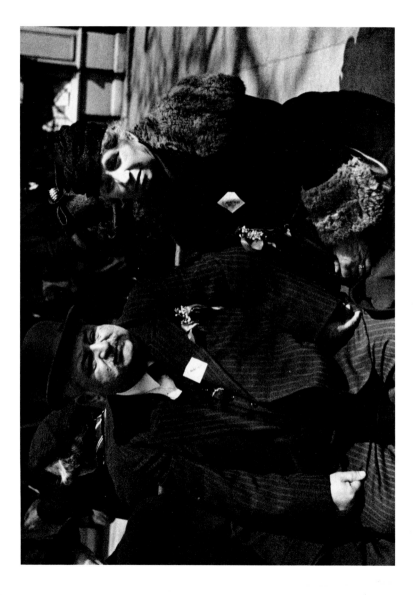

6. Veterans of World War I, France, 1936.

7. Veterans of World War I, Verdun, 1937.

8. Madrid, July 1936.

9. Spain, 1936.

10. Spain, 1937.

11. Spain, November 1936.
Overleaf: Teruel, December 24, 1937.

13. Death of a Republican soldier, Spain, near Cerro Muriano, about
September 5, 1936.

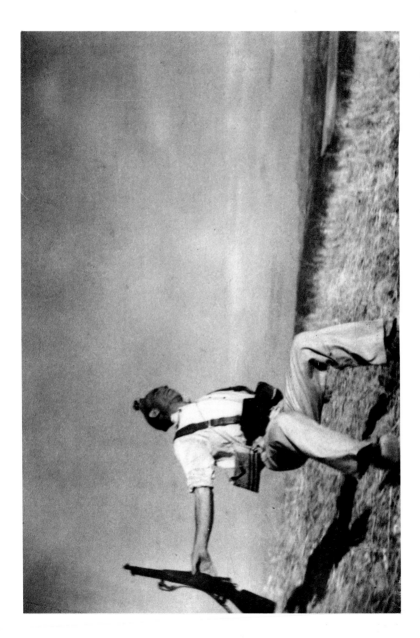

14. Spain, near Fraga, November 7, 1938.

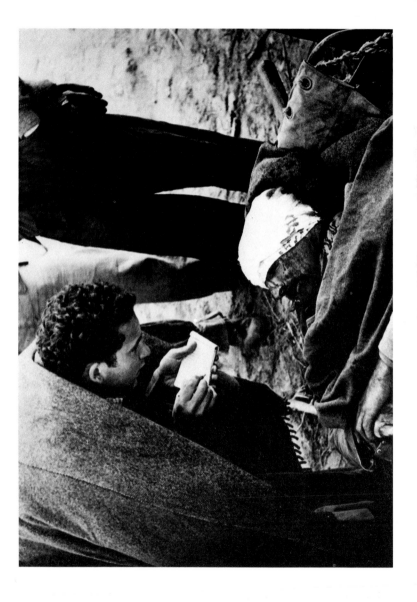

15. Mexico, July 7, 1940.

16. Spain, 1937.

17. Bilbao, May 1937.

18. Bilbao, May 1937.

19. Madrid, 1936.

20. Farewell ceremonies for the volunteers of the International Brigades, near Barcelona, October 25, 1938.

21. Transfer of Spanish Republican refugees between Argelès-sur-Mer and Barcarès, France, March 1939.

22. China, near the Xuzhou front, April 1938.

23. Canton, July-August 1938.

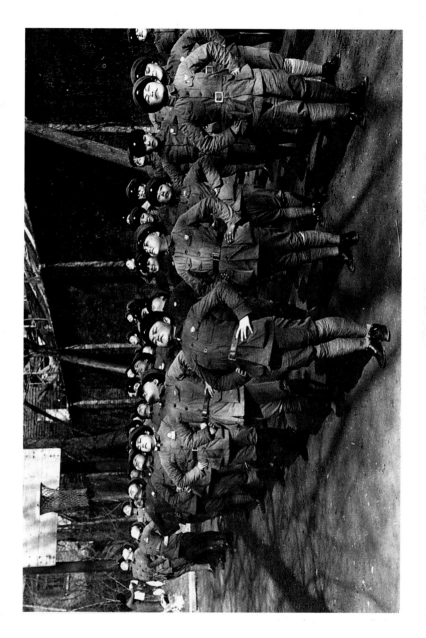

24. Ferryboat on the Yellow River, China, April-September 1938.

25. After an air raid, Hankow, China, July-September 1938.

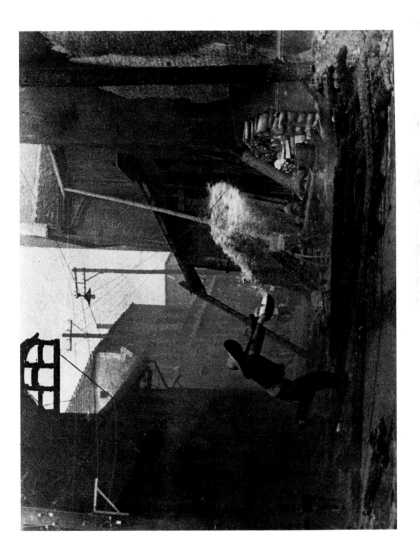

26. Hankow, China, July-September 1938.
Overleaf: The Tour de France in Pleyben, Brittany, July 1939.

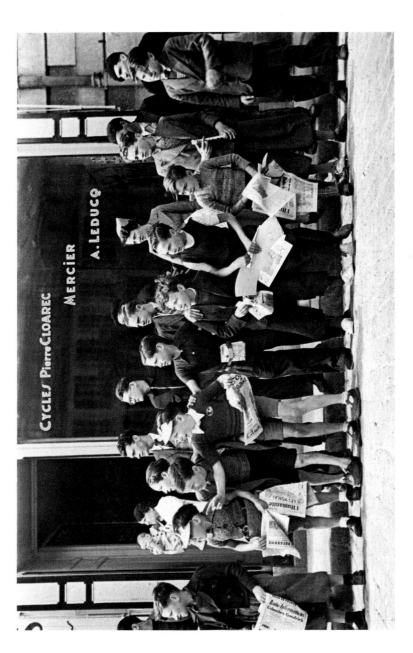

29. Calumet City, Illinois, December 1940.

30. Italy, October 1943.

31. Troina, Sicily, August 6, 1943.

32. Monreale, Sicily, 1943.

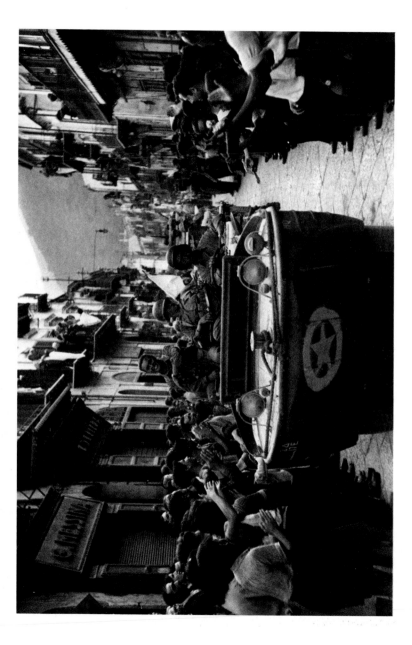

33. On the road from Naples, about September 30, 1943.

34. Sicily, 1943.

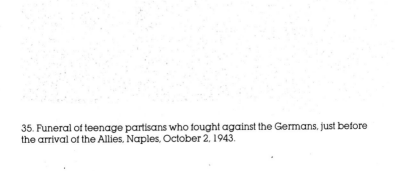

35. Funeral of teenage partisans who fought against the Germans, just before the arrival of the Allies, Naples, October 2, 1943.

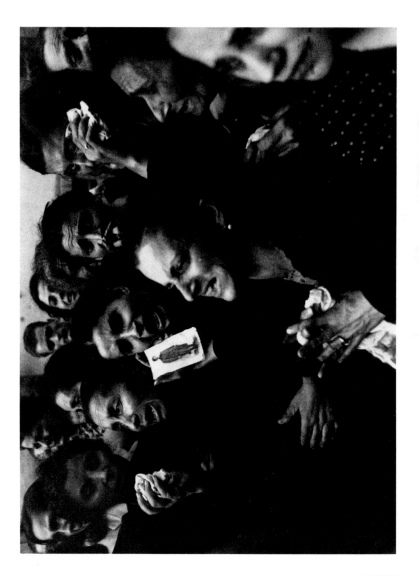

36. Naples, October 2, 1943.
Overleaf: Landing of American troops on the Normandy coast, Omaha Beach, June 6, 1944.

39. Omaha Beach, June 6, 1944.

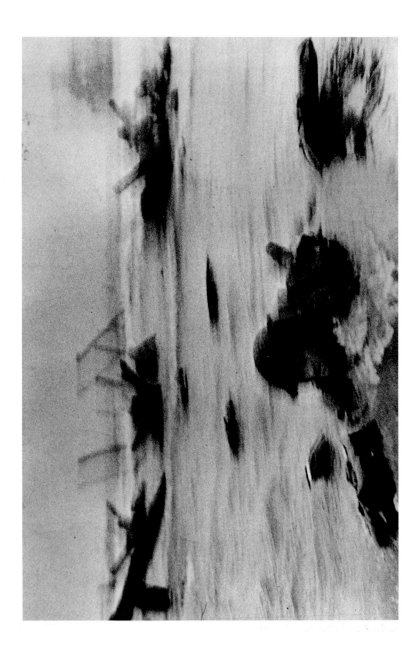

40. After the landing, Omaha Beach, June 1944.

41. Notre-Dame-de-Cenilly, southwest of Saint-Lô, July 28, 1944.

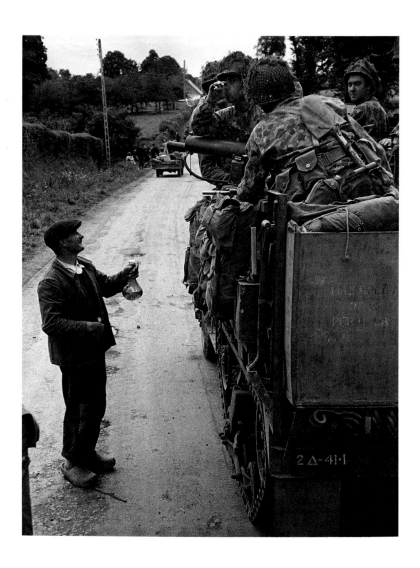

42. Normandy, July 26-30, 1944.

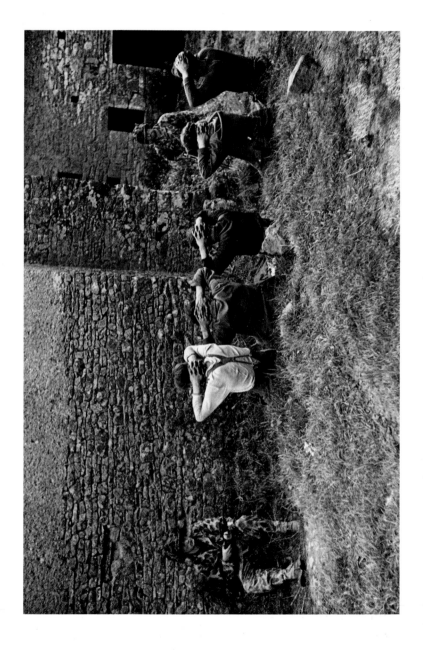

43. Paris, August 25, 1944.

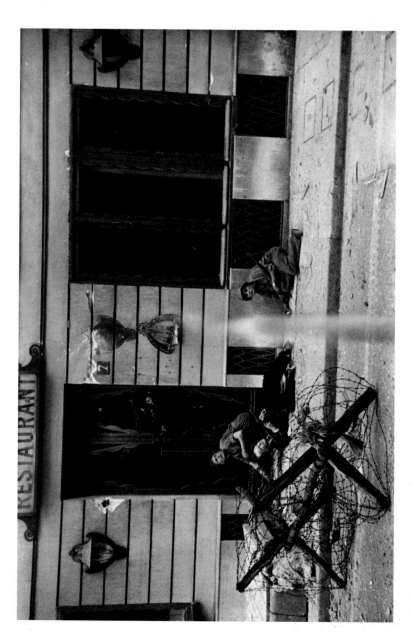

44. Chartres, August 18, 1944.
Overleaf: Chartres, August 18, 1944.

46. Paris, August 25, 1944.

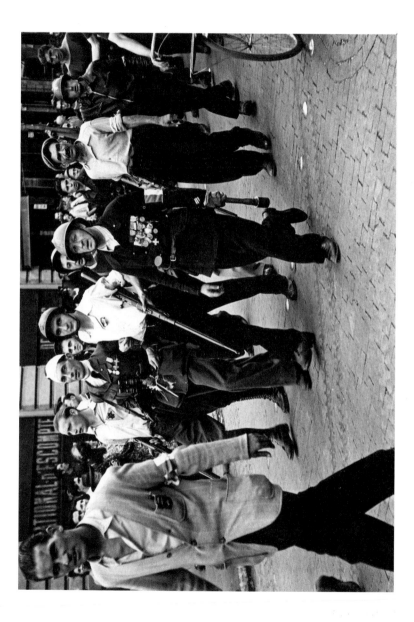

47. Paris, August 26, 1944.
Overleaf: Paris, August 26, 1944.

49. Paris, August 26, 1944.

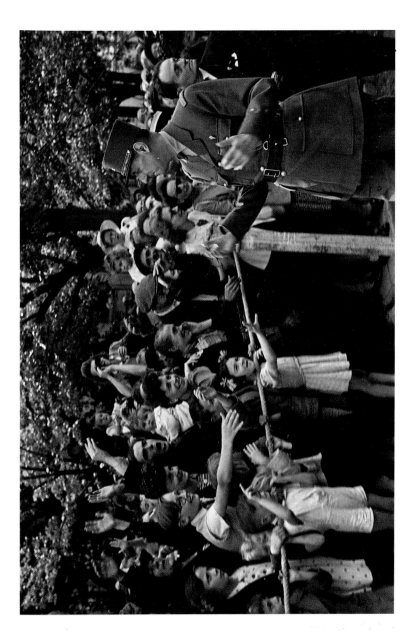

50: Alençon, August 12, 1944.

51. Germany, 1945.

52. Belgium, south of Bastogne, December 23-26, 1944.

53. Germany, near Wesel, March 24, 1945.

54. Germany, near Wesel, March 24, 1945.

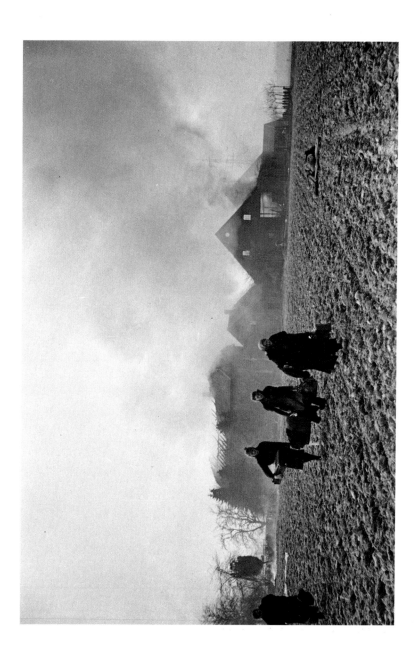

55. Ghetto ruins, Warsaw, October 1948.

56-59. Death of an American soldier, Leipzig, April 18, 1945.

60. Refugee camp in Haifa, Israel, 1949.

61. Refugee camp near Haifa, Israel, October-November 1950.
Overleaf: Tel Aviv, June 22, 1948, and May 1949.

64. Village of blind immigrants, south of Tel Aviv, November-December 1950.

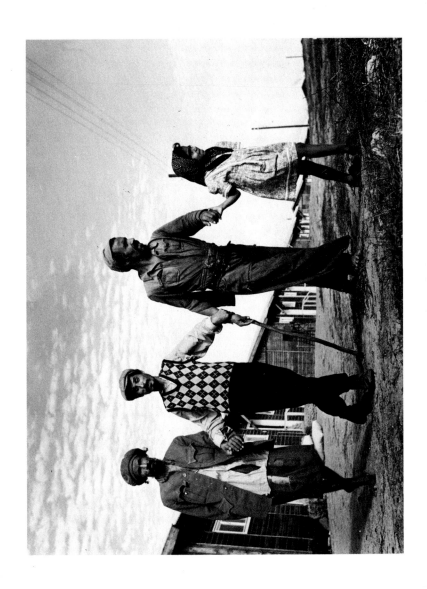

65. Nam Dinh, May 21, 1954.

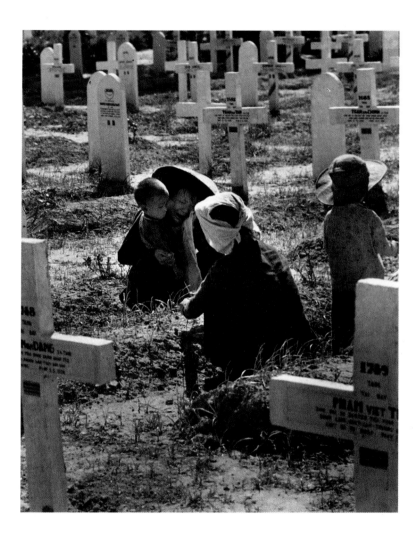

66. On the road to Thai Binh, Indochina, May 25, 1954.

67. On the road to Thai Binh, Indochina, May 25, 1954.

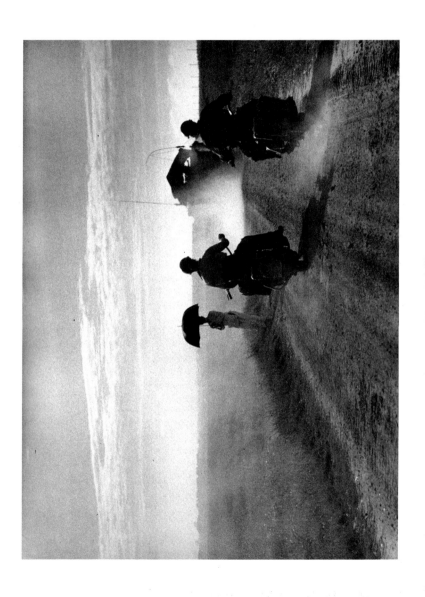

68. On the road to Thai-Binh (Robert Capa's last photograph), Indochina, May 25, 1954.

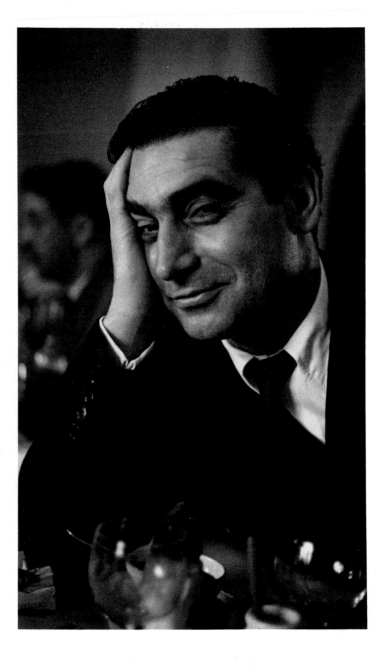

BIOGRAPHY

compiled by Stuart Alexander

1913. Born Endre Ernö Friedmann on October 22 in Budapest.

1930. Begins to photograph.

1931. Works as a photographer for Ullstein, Ltd., in Berlin, and for the Dephot photography agency.

1931-33. Studies political science at the Deutsche Hochschule für Politik in Berlin.

1933-35. Moves to Paris, where he struggles to find work. Meets Henri Cartier-Bresson, David "Chim" Seymour, and Gerda Taro. Makes innumerable contacts that will be invaluable to him later when starting the Magnum agency. Participates in the founding of the Alliance Photo Agency, run by Maria Eisner, who later became the secretary-treasurer of the fledgling Magnum agency. Takes the name André Friedmann.

1935. Takes the name Robert Capa and begins his collaboration with Gerda Taro.

1936. Photographs the Spanish Civil War. His work is published regularly in *Vu, Regards, Ce Soir, Weekly Illustrated* (London), *Life*, and various other magazines. Begins his career as a news photographer.

1937. Death of Gerda Taro in Spain.

1938. Works in China.

1939. Emigrates to the United States, where his mother lives in New York.

1941-45. Photographs World War II as a European correspondent for *Life* magazine. Throughout the war, his work appears regularly in the *Illustrated* (London) and *Collier's*.

1947. Receives the Freedom Medal from the U.S. Army. Starts Magnum Photos with Henri Cartier-Bresson, George Rodger, and Chim Seymour. Writes his first book, *Slightly Out of Focus*. Travels in Russia with John Steinbeck.

1948-50. Works in Israel.

1949. Shoots his first sequences for *Holiday* magazine.

1951. Becomes president of Magnum.

1954. Becomes a naturalized American citizen. While on assignment for *Life* magazine, steps on a land mine at Thai Binh in Indochina (Vietnam) and is killed. The French army posthumously awards him the Croix de Guerre.

1955. The Overseas Press Club and *Life* magazine establish the annual Robert Capa Prize.

Capa's archives are maintained by Magnum, and by the International Center of Photography in New York.

Robert Capa by Ruth Orkin

BIBLIOGRAPHY

Books by and about Capa

1938. Death in the Making, by Robert Capa. Photographs by Robert Capa and Gerda Taro, captions by Gerda Taro, preface by Jay Allen, art direction by André Kertész. Covici-Friede. 149 photographs.

1941. The Battle of Waterloo Road, by Diana Forbes-Robertson and Robert Capa. Random House, New York.

1944. Invasion!, by Charles Christian Wertenbaker. Photographs by Robert Capa. Appleton-Century, New York and London.

1947. Slightly Out of Focus, by Robert Capa. Henry Holt, New York. 121 photographs. Japanese edition published in 1956.

1948. A Russian Journal, by John Steinbeck. Photographs by Robert Capa. Viking, New York. 70 photographs.

1950. Report on Israel, by Irwin Shaw and Robert Capa. Photographs by Robert Capa. Simon and Schuster, New York. 94 photographs.

1960. Robert Capa: War Photographs, by Jozefa Stuart. Introduction by John Steinbeck. Smithsonian Institution, Washington, D.C. 18 photographs.

1964. Images of War, by Robert Capa. Grossman, New York. 94 photographs. Also French, Italian, German, and Japanese editions.

1969. Robert Capa. Edited by Anna Farova. Text by several authors. Paragraphic Books/Grossman, New York. 60 photographs.

1974. Robert Capa, 1913-1954. Introduction by Cornell Capa, I.C.P. Grossman, New York. 93 photographs.

1976. Front Populaire, by Robert Capa and David "Chim" Seymour. Text by Georgette Elgey. Chene/Magnum, Paris. 44 photographs by Robert Capa.

1976. Capa: Emlèkkiállitás. Introduction by Ivan Boldiszár. Budapest Mucsarnok, Budapest. 10 photographs.

1979. Robert Capa, by Romeo Martinez. Mondadori, Milan. 108 photographs.

1980. Les Grandes Photos de la guerre d'Espagne. Text by Georges Goria. Photographs by Robert Capa and David "Chim" Seymour. Jannink, Paris. 80 photographs by Capa.

1980. Robert Capa. Pacific Press Service, Tokyo, and the International Center of Photography, New York. Over 260 photographs.

1983. Robert Capa. Text by Anna Winand. Fabbri, Milan. 67 photographs.

1984. Robert Capa: War and Peace. Pacific Press Services, Tokyo, and the International Center of Photography, New York. 19 color photographs, 280 black-and-white.

1985. Robert Capa: Photographs. Edited by Richard Whelan and Cornell Capa. Knopf, New York. 262 photographs. Also French and Italian editions.

1985. Robert Capa: A Biography, by Richard Whelan. Knopf, New York. (French translation: Mazarine, Paris, 1985.)

1986. Robert Capa. Fundacio Caixa de Pensions, Barcelona. 21 photographs.

1986. Robert Capa: Sommertage,

Friedenstage: Berlin 1945. Edited by Diethart Kerbs. Photographs by Robert Capa. Dirk Nishen/Verlag in Kreuzberg, Berlin. 30 photographs.

1987. Robert Capa: Cuadernos de Guerra en España (1936-1939). Edited by Carlos Serrano. Salla Parpalló/IVEI, Valencia. 67 photographs, 45 pages of facsimile reproductions from journals, 6 photographs by Gerda Taro.

Other books

1968. The Concerned Photographer. Edited and with an introduction by Cornell Capa. Text by Robert Sagalyn and Judith Friedberg. Grossman, New York. 26 photographs by Capa.

1969. Israel, The Reality: People, Places, Events in Memorable Photographs. Edited by Cornell Capa. Preface by Nelson Glueck. Introduction by Moshe Shamir. World Publishing, in association with the Jewish Museum, New York. 4 photographs by Capa.

1971. Photojournalism. Life Library of Photography, Time-Life Books, New York, pp. 66-67.

1972. Behind the Great Wall of China: Photographs from 1870 to the Present. Edited by Cornell Capa. Introduction by Weston J. Naef. Metropolitan Museum of Art, New York. 16 photographs by Capa.

1973. Looking at Photographs, by John Szarkowski. Museum of Modern Art, New York, pp. 145-46. 1 photograph by Capa.

1981. "Views of Paris: Notes on a Parisian," by Irwin Shaw. In **Paris/ Magnum: Photographs 1935-1981.** Introduction by Inge Morath. Aperture, New York. Text on Capa, pp. 11-17. 4 photographs by Capa.

1986. "Death in the Making: Representing the Spanish Civil War," by David Mellor. In **No Pasaran! Photographs and Posters of the**

Spanish Civil War. Arnolfini Gallery, Bristol, England, pp. 24-43. 7 photographs by Capa.

Periodicals

"Capa's Camera," *Time*, February 28, 1938.

"This Is War," *Picture Post*, vol. 1, no. 10. December 3, 1938, pp. 13-24. Cover and 18 photographs.

"Coal Mine Characters by Capa," *U.S. Camera*, June 1943.

"The Man Who Invented Himself," by John Hersey. *'47: The Magazine of the Year*, September 1947.

"Women and Children in the USSR," by John Steinbeck and Robert Capa. *Ladies' Home Journal*, vol. 65, no. 2 (February 1948), pp. 44-59. Cover, 14 color photographs, 34 black-and-white.

"From the Rubble," by Theodore H. White. *Holiday*, vol. 5, no. 6 (June 1949), pp. 80-81, 83-86, 88-89, 142-45. 12 photographs.

"Robert Capa, Werner Bischof," by John G. Morris. *Infinity*, May 1954, pp. 3-7. Cover and 4 photographs.

"Adieu Capa," by Louis Aragon. *Les lettres françaises*, May 27-June 3, 1954.

"A Farewell to Two Photographers: A Last Salute to Two Men," *Camera*, vol. 33, no. 6 (June 1954), pp. 283-84.

"A Great War Reporter and His Last Battle," *Life*, vol. 36, no. 23 (June 7, 1954), pp. 27-30, 7 photographs.

"He Said: 'This Is Going to Be a Beautiful Story.'" by John Mecklin. *Life*, vol. 36, no. 23 (June 7, 1954), pp. 31-33. 6 photographs.

"Death Stops the Shutter," *Time*, June 7, 1954.

"Capa and Bischof... They Were Two

Great Photographers," *Photography* (London), vol. 9, no. 7 (July 1954), pp. 44-48. 4 photographs by Capa. (Also see pp. 22, 24.)

"Robert Capa, 1913-1954/Werner Bischof, 1915-1954," by Jacquelyn Judge. *Modern Photography*, vol. 18, no. 8 (August 1954), pp. 42-43, 87-88. 1 photograph.

"Robert Capa": An Appreciation," by John Steinbeck. *Popular Photography*, vol. 35, no. 3 (September 1954), pp. 48-53. 8 photographs.

"A Man Named Capa," by Al Silverman. *Saga*, February 1958, pp. 22-25, 72-75. 5 photographs.

"Robert Capa," by Nelson Gidding. *Camera*, vol. 40, no. 3 (March 1961), pp. 5-25. 25 photographs and cover, in color. Text by John Steinbeck and Ernest Hemingway.

"The Many Faces of War," *New York Times Magazine*, April 19, 1964, pp. 30-31. 8 photographs.

"Images of War: Robert Capa: A Review," by W. Eugene Smith. *Infinity*, vol. 13, no. 7 (July 1964), pp. 4-10. 8 photographs.

"Robert Capa," *Camera*, vol. 48, no. 5 (May 1969). pp. 2-8. 6 photographs.

"Omaggio a Bob Capa," by Lanfranco Colombo. *Fotografia Italiana*, no. 173 (June 1972), pp. 18-64. 112 photographs. Text by Piero Berengo Gardin.

"Robert Capa," *Creative Camera*, no. 108 (June 1973), pp. 190-201. 12 photographs and cover.

"My Friend Capa," by György Markos. *The New Hungarian Quaterly*, Winter 1976.

"Capa: le mythe vivant," *Photo* (Paris),

no. 143 (August 1979), pp. 48-59, 109. 11 photographs.

"Les amis de Capa: Gary Cooper et Hemingway vus par Robert Capa lors du tournage de 'Pour qui sonne le glas,'" *Photo* (Paris), no. 155 (August 1980), pp. 14-21, 81. 13 photographs.

"Forgotten Pictures of the Spanish Civil War: Photographs by Robert Capa, David Seymour, and Gerda Taro," by Arthur Goldsmith. *Camera Arts*, vol. 1, no. 2 (March/April 1981), pp. 62-71, 101-102. 6 photographs by Capa.

"End Paper: Moment of Truth," by Arthur Goldsmith. *Camera Arts*, vol. 1, no. 2 (March/April 1981), pp. 111-14. 2 photographs. Article on the photo of the death of a Spanish soldier.

"Robert Capa: 124 photos retrouvées," *Photo* (Paris), no. 189 (June 1983), pp. 72-85, 114. 29 photographs, 5 illustrations.

"The Capa Caper," by David Markus. *American Photographer*, vol. 2, no. 4 (October 1983), pp. 90-95. 5 photographs, 2 illustrations. Article on the rediscovery of Capa's photographs.

"Robert Capa," *Photo Japan* (Tokyo), no. 005 (March 1984), pp. 123-45. 42 photographs, 6 illustrations.

"Capa: The Man Behind the Myth," by Richard Whelan. *American Photographer*, vol. 15, no. 4 (October 1985), pp. 43-57. 1 color photograph, 16 black-and-white.

"Capa par Capa," *Photo* (Paris), no. 217 (October 1985), pp. 90-97, 136. 8 photographs.

"Essay-Review," by Steve Cagan. *Exposure* (Society for Photographic Education), vol. 24, no. 2 (Summer 1986), pp. 36-42.

EXHIBITIONS

Main Solo Exhibitions

1952. "On Picasso," Museum of Modern Art, New York. (With Gjon Mili.)

1960. "Robert Capa: War Photographs," Smithsonian Institution, Washington, D.C. (Traveling exhibition which went around the world, 1960-1965.)

1964. "Images of War," Smithsonian Institution, Washington, D.C.

1966. "A Magyar Fotomúvészet 125-év," Magyar Nemzeti Galéria, Budapest.

1976. "Capa: Emlékkiállitás," Budapest Mucsarnok, Budapest.

1980. "Robert Capa," Tokyo.

1982. "Robert Capa: War and Peace," Tokyo.

1985. "Robert Capa: Photographs," International Center of Photography, New York.

1986. Fundacio Caixa de Pensions, Barcelona.

1987. Sala Parpallo, Valencia, Spain.

Main Group Exhibitions

1951. "Memorable Life Photographs," Museum of Modern Art, New York.

1955. "The Family of Man," Museum of Modern Art, New York.

1960. "The World as Seen by Magnum Photographers," Smithsonian Institution, Washington, D.C.

1964. "The Photographer's Eye," Museum of Modern Art, New York.

1968. "The Concerned Photographer," Riverside Museum, New York.

1969. "Israel: The Reality," Jewish Museum, New York.

1972. "Behind the Great Wall of China," Metropolitan Museum, New York.

1973. "Looking at Photographs," Museum of Modern Art, New York.

1974. "The Classics of Documentary Photography," International Center of Photography, New York.

1981. "Spain 1936-1939," International Center of Photography, New York.

1986. "No Pasaran! Photographs and Posters of the Spanish Civil War," Arnolfini Gallery, Bristol, England.

FILMS

1938. *The Four Hundred Million*, by Joris Ivens. (Capa was the second cameraman.)

1946. *The March of Time* (Turkey). Direction: Robert Capa. Photography: Paul Martellière.

1948. 8 films on Paris fashion. World Video, New York.

1948. *The Journey* (on Israel). United Jewish Appeal, New York. Direction: Robert Capa. Production: John Fernhout. Photography: Jacques Letellier.

PANTHEON PHOTO LIBRARY

American Photographers of the Depression
Eugène Atget
Brassaï
Robert Capa
Henri Cartier-Bresson
Bruce Davidson
Early Color Photography
Robert Frank
Lee Friedlander
André Kertész
Jacques-Henri Lartigue
Duane Michals
Helmut Newton
The Nude
Man Ray
Alexander Rodchenko
W. Eugene Smith
Weegee

The Pantheon Photo Library:
a collection conceived and produced by the
National Center of Photography in Paris
under the direction of Robert Delpire.